i

Would you like to pray in tongues … you can!

Ben Emet.

Unless otherwise stated all Bible references are taken from:

The Holy Bible; New King James Version © 1982 by Thomas Nelson, Inc. English Standard Version © 2010 by Crossway. New American Standard Bible © 1960, 1962, 1963, 1968, 1971, 1972, 1973, 1975, 1977, 1995 by The Lockman Foundation. New International Version © 1973, 1978, 1984 by Biblica, Inc. The Amplified Bible, Expanded Edition © AMP © 1987 by Zondervan and The Lockman Foundation. The Complete Jewish Bible © 1998 by Jewish New Testament Publications, Inc. The Living Bible © 2005 by Tyndale House Publishers, Inc. Good News Bible © 1976 by American Bible Society. The Message © 1993, 1994, 1995 by NavPress.

Contents

		Page
Introduction		v
A.	The importance of the spoken word	1
B.	The Gift of the Holy Spirit comes with His own gifts	3
C.	Divisive yet inclusive	5
D.	Praying in tongues circumvents our own thoughts or mind on matters	7
E.	What does Paul teach on this matter?	8
F.	So, how do you take a hold of it?	10
G.	Some fundamental statements	13
H.	Some benefits of speaking/praying in tongues	15
Bibliography		16

Introduction.

There has been a huge amount of controversy surrounding this Biblical aspect of Christian living. As a person who has been ministering in this area for more than 30 years and seeing phenomenal grace and results, I thought it prudent to pass on the fundamentals concerning this doctrine. The truth about Kingdom matters will always be Spirit-driven and therefore it will be creative and bring life.

This exposition will be a bit like doing a jigsaw puzzle, getting the outer framework together, and then it will be easier to fill in the rest of the picture. Ultimately, once it has all come together, the complete picture can then be enjoyed. Hopefully, once you have read and understand the principles involved, you will be able to take a hold of the promise of God and enjoy a personal, direct line of prayer to God.

The most common questions I've encountered are:

1. Why should speaking in tongues be important to me, I have other divine gifts in operation in my life?

2. Is "speaking in tongues" available to all believers or only to an elect group? In practical terms, can I speak in tongues? As a gift from God (Acts 2:38); is it God's choice to bless some Christians exclusively, or can all Christians take a hold of His gift – in other words, is it available to me? This is an important question, as it addresses God's intention for speaking or praying in

tongues; as well as the divisiveness of assigning tongues to the select special few, like Apostle Paul, who prayed in tongues more than anyone else!

Before answering these questions directly let's start with some fundamental statements or principles.

A. The importance of the spoken word:

1. The Creative power of the spoken word:

When we speak our words are creative. God creates by what He "says". Genesis1:3, 6, 9, 11, 14, 20, 24, 29, all says: "And God said…" And in 2 Corinthians 4:6 "For it is God who commanded, who said, 'Let light shine out of darkness...'". God made the eternal spiritual and created the temporal physical by pronouncing, speaking, proclaiming "Let there be..." Genesis is clear God spoke things into being. He could have just "thought it" into being, there was no one else was around, but He spoke it into being – He set the principle down eternally: we translate the spiritual into the natural, our thoughts into reality, by what we verbalise or speak.

2. Jesus, is the "Word", He is the physical expressed image of the unseen invisible God.

He is the Word that was made flesh and dwelt among us (John 1:1) – The Word being God! Who then was made manifest and dwelt with us. The Word, not the idea or the act, but the Word. Again, as the Word, He represents the physical manifestation of the "spoken" yet living "Word".

3. This principle is also foundational to our salvation. Our spiritual reality is affirmed by what we say, the confession of our faith.

We believe in our hearts and confess with our mouth unto salvation. "If you declare with your mouth, 'Jesus is Lord,' and believe in your heart that God raised him from the dead, you will be saved. For it is with your heart that you believe and are justified, and it is with your mouth that you profess your faith and are saved." (Romans 10: 8-10).

4. Verbal prayer is so important, when Jesus taught the disciples how to pray, He taught them first to vocalise, that is, to pray aloud, and to say, "Our Father who are in heaven...." And He actively encouraged His disciples to ask for the gift of Holy Spirit, who would enable them to pray more effectively (Luke 11:2-13). That in itself is curious, even while they were walking with Jesus they still had to personally ask for Holy Spirit to assist them in their prayers!

5. David often advocated verbal (spoken) prayer (e.g. Psalm 5; 142:1).

6. The natural mirrors the spiritual. All thoughts are given substance by what we say, i.e. what I think is made understandable by saying it aloud. I won't accurately know what you are thinking until you share it with me by telling me what you are thinking about. Also, think about the power of simple speech – when we speak we transmit sound waves – it is unstoppable! Your voice always moves the listener's eardrums! That is physical power you exert by just speaking to someone! Your voice releases physical power, how much more so when it is Holy Spirit driven?

B. The Gift of the Holy Spirit (δορεα) comes with His own gifts (Χαρισματα).

1. In Acts we see repeatedly that "speaking in tongues" was the sign that the people had received Holy Spirit. In Acts 10:45-46 we have the clearest example, "And those of the circumcision who believed were astonished, as many as came with Peter, because the gift (δορεα) of the Holy Spirit had been poured out on the Gentiles also. FOR they heard them speak with tongues and (και) magnify God." Many try to change the and into "or", do not be fooled, or enticed, the Greek is very clear! So too when the Ephesians came to faith, they had already received the Holy Spirit and they were baptised; yet afterwards Paul still laid hands on them and Holy Spirit came upon them (ερχομαι – made his appearance in public and dynamically empowering them) and they (too) spoke with tongues and (και) prophesied. Acts 19:6, "And when Paul had laid his hands upon them, the Holy Spirit came on them, and they began speaking with tongues and prophesying."

2. Tongues are one of the signs promised to those who believe and are baptised in Mark 16:16-17. Jesus said, "He who has believed and has been baptized shall be saved; but he who has disbelieved shall be condemned. These miraculous signs will accompany those who believe: They will cast out demons in my name, and they will speak in new languages. They will be able to handle snakes with safety, and if they drink anything poisonous, it won't hurt them. They will be able to place their hands

3

on the sick, and they will be healed." Jesus, God Himself, said very clearly "the one believing" shall speak in tongues (γλοσαα - tongues: defined as "of uncertain affinity; the tongue; by implication, a language [specially, one naturally unacquired]: - tongue."). Literally "their tongues will speak". All who believe and is baptised. We do not even have the same clarity of our mandate in the great commission where one can argue that it was addressed only to the disciples or hearers. Here He was more direct – the ones believing will speak in tongues! Take note! Jesus said so. The Ancient of Days, not just an apostle, but the Great Apostle stated it clearly as a sign for all believers.

C. Even though the Gospel is divisive - it is utterly inclusive – "speaking in tongues" follows exactly the same divine pattern.

Jesus is the only way to Father-God, believe in Him and you will be saved - He is "available" to all. Jesus once and for all time paid the price for all who would be willing to believe in Him (John 6:29). And, "The Lord is not slow about His promise, as some count slowness, but is patient toward you, not wishing for any to perish but for all to come to repentance." However, "Our lives are a Christ-like fragrance rising up to God. But this fragrance is perceived differently by those who are being saved and by those who are perishing. To those who are perishing, we are a dreadful smell of death and doom. But to those who are being saved, we are a life-giving perfume!" The message of empowering prayer in the Spirit follows the same pattern. To teach that tongues are just for a select few is very divisive, for we all need to be edified or built up; and by implication it would mean that only a chosen few will be empowered to grow. Paul's discourse in 1 Corinthians 14 can best be understood when we use the same template for brushing teeth and flossing teeth. When Paul asks whether all speak in tongues it is the equivalent to "do all of us brush our teeth"? I would much rather you all prophesy, which would equate to "I would rather you all floss"! They are not mutually exclusive! He is using a hebraism to stress the importance of prophecy. In fact, Paul wants everyone to speak in tongues and everyone to prophesy. King Solomon already inferred that all of God's children should speak His mind (Proverbs 22:20-21). His language needs to be understood in terms of the context of what he is trying to stress, "earnestly desire the spiritual gifts", all of them! But start with tongues and step into prophecy – for all can attain to these two. "Eagerly pursue and seek to acquire [this] love [make it your aim, your great quest]; and earnestly desire and cultivate the spiritual endowments (gifts), especially that you may prophesy (interpret the divine will and purpose in inspired preaching and teaching)". (AMP, 1Corinthians 14:1).

D. Praying or speaking in tongues circumvents our own thoughts or mind on matters.

It is a gift from the Gift. The Father's promise or primary gift is Holy Spirit. And in this matter, the most important thing to remember at all times is that it is always about Holy Spirit praying through us, so that we become a conduit for Him. The gift prevents our own minds and thoughts interfering in our prayers to God, for when we do so we pray from the heart. As we pray in tongues, we have the full assurance of that creative power we have explained earlier, "the word that goes forth from My mouth (now through your mouth): it shall not return void unto Me, but it shall accomplish what I please. And it shall prosper in the thing for which l sent it." (Isaiah 55:10-11).

Golgotha was the place where Jesus was crucified. The "place of the skull", the battle is always for our minds and hearts. In Acts 2 we read about the day of Pentecost, "And there appeared to them tongues ($\gamma\lambda\sigma\sigma\alpha\iota$) [not an arm, leg, brain, eye, ear or any other organ or limb!] as of fire distributing themselves, and they rested on each one of them. And they were all filled with the Holy Spirit and began to speak with other tongues, as the Spirit was giving them utterance." Tongues of fire to induces speaking in tongues! While praying in tongues Holy Spirit can circumvent our heads (mind and/or soulish thinking) and He comes as a tongue! Settling on each one of them (now us).

E. What does Paul teach on this matter?

There is a difference between "speaking in tongues" and the "gift" of tongues, but a bit more on this later.

Tongues as a gift from God, might not seem as spectacular as the other gifts, but yet it is a wonderful gift from God and at the very least we are told to "... earnestly desire and cultivate the spiritual gifts." (1 Corinthians 14:1). He continues in verse 2, "He who speaks in a [strange] tongue edifies (builds up) and improves himself." (AMP). Paul himself professes that he still needs to pray in tongues as he still needs spiritual edification and wrote, "I thank my God that I pray in tongues more than any of you." (1 Corinthians 14:18). By implication, if Paul needed to speak in tongues to be continually edified, then surely we do too. As far as circumventing one's own mind and thoughts Paul reiterates that very clearly, "For one who speaks in an [unknown] tongue speaks not unto men but to God {this is key}, for no one {not even he himself!!} understands or catches his meaning, because in the [Holy] Spirit he utters secret truths and hidden things [not obvious to the understanding]." 1 Corinthians 14:2 (AMP). When you pray in tongues no-one can understand you – but God! You are talking "mysteries" to Him. Paul then writes that praying or speaking in tongues immediately encourages two of the other Holy Spirit's gifts (apart from improving your personal worship straight away). His teaching continued, "Let him who speaks in a tongue pray that he may interpret." Once he does, he can interpret for others and in so doing he is prophesying! (Verse 5). And in verse 15, concerning worship, "I will sing in the spirit while singing with understanding (in my thoughts) at the very same time". There is simultaneous worship on two levels for those who worship in tongues.

Speaking in tongues as a sign of Holy Spirit comes with a wonderful promise and divine assurance. When Jesus taught His disciples to pray in Luke 11, He did so in four bits. The first being the "Our Father in heaven", the second is about intercession, the third is about breakthrough in prayer (ask, seek, knock) and the fourth is about involving Holy Spirit in prayer. Jesus promised that if you ask for bread, Father-God will not give you a stone (or earthly, inert or dead thing) and if you ask for a fish or an egg He will not give you a snake or a scorpion. In other words, when you sincerely ask Father-God for Holy Spirit (to assist you in prayer), He will not allow the Enemy (the Devil or demonic) to usurp your need and He assures you that it will not come from yourself! You will not be making it up! In practical simple terms, if you step out in faith, and you speak, it transcends you, the tongue will become alive – Holy Spirit empowered – and that is God's promise.

The gift of tongues Paul explained is when the tongue is understood by unbelievers who knows you cannot their language (Acts 2:11-12, 1 Corinthians 14:22-25).

F. SO, HOW DO YOU TAKE A HOLD OF IT?

1. Be hungry and thirsty for Him and His gift – (Also read John 7:37-38).

2. Be an open conduit -- Forgive, forgive and forgive. If you are unwilling to gift another person and refusing to show mercy … it might become a stumbling block when you want a gracious, merciful gift from God. Forgive and clear all debts and then receive God's gracious gift with willingness of heart. In this respect forgiveness is key, not only for salvation, but for Holy Spirit to operate freely in and through your life. (Matthew 18:21-35).

3. Ask sincerely to receive the gift and rely on the faithfulness and goodness of God (Luke 11:13). Faith is the substance of things hoped for. You know you will be doing the speaking while Holy Spirit does the empowering– speaking mysteries to God that even you don't understand, but you're doing so from deep inside, from your heart. "And they were all filled with the Holy Spirit and [they] began to speak with other tongues, as the Spirit was giving them utterance." The "giving utterance" in context means as Holy Spirit prompted or nudged you from within to speak forth. The deep desire to speak out – to burst forth comes from you and is encouraged by Him. That is why there has to be a sincere desire for it! He comes and releases the dam for the river to burst forth. But you do the speaking, the making of the sounds of the tongue.

4. If you are still struggling to take a hold of it, seek out someone who loves to pray in tongues incessantly and ask them to lay hands on you and pray for you and with you.

5. Then just start, do not think about what to say; just start to speak to God from your heart! As already said, even in Acts 2, they started speaking as the Spirit gave utterance.

(a) Start vocalising – make any sound and He will add the utterance – it is that simple! Gobbledygook with a prayerful, reverential attitude towards God!

(b) Remember "without faith it is impossible to please God..." that is the step of faith that's required here; trust that He is involved and then just start ... and rivers of living water will gush out of your innermost being. You will find the promised refreshing and invariably a new desire to glorify God and to intercede for those around you.

6. Tongues "God-focuses" you; heart-directed tongues in dialogue with God 24/7 not only builds you up, but makes you actively reach out to God and His presence continually.

7. Do not give up, if not at first, pursue and pursue and receive His grace, it is for you -- believe it, receive it.

8. You must be aware, that as salvation, there are obstacles to overcome.

(a) The first one is that it will feel and sound very awkward. You might even be tempted to believe that you're making it up! And, yes in fact you are! But the promise is the transcendence of Holy Spirit, using your voice as that creative force and that nothing will return void unto you for God has promised that as long as you use it, He will step on board and utilise your voice as a voice for Him. Holy Spirit interceding on our behalf! You cannot lose.

(b) Feeling awkward? Disregard it and continue to step out in faith, believing the Word of God more than your feelings. Did not Jesus promise "I will ask the Father, and He will give you another Helper, that He may be with you forever"! Allow Him to speak through you.

(c) Remember, with God it is always about grace, not works or how you perform, that is why it is so simple, so wonderfully easy. Start now, just give it a go, just do it!

G. SOME FUNDAMENTAL STATEMENTS:

1. God is always good; and He is our good Father.

2. As our good Father it is His good pleasure to give us good gifts and His Kingdom.

3. We receive His gifts through faith – Salvation (Ephesians 2: 8, 9, John 6: 2) and Holy Spirit (δορεα - Galatians 3:2).

4. God's creative power is most clearly demonstrated by what He says. (Genesis 1; Isaiah 55:10-11; John. 1:1). We too can, in collaborating with Holy Spirit, demonstrate His creative power by what we say.

5. Tongues is the gift that enables the creative power of Holy Spirit from within as we speak mysteries unto God. By it we're edified and by it we worship God.

6. No gift from God is "lesser" and we should earnestly desire them all.

7. "Tongues" in Acts is frequently the "entry" gift and is confirmation or sign to those who exercised it of the Promise of Holy Spirit as in Mark 16:16.

8. Receiving God's gifts through faith must of essence be simple and easy as it is made available to all - i.e. the Gospel and Holy Spirit are completely accessible and inclusive.

9. Tongues will edify (build up) every believer who exercises it.

10. Tongues is NOT a sign of Christianity, nor of hosting Holy Spirit; it is a gift not *the* gift; Holy Spirit is the Gift we all receive when we believe in Jesus Christ as our Saviour.

11. It is divisive to teach that tongues are only for a select few, those who are too weak and who need tongues to be edified; effectively, if the practical conclusion is drawn, then only those who are more 'spiritual' or closer to God than Paul will not need tongues, as he was thanking God for his ability to use it perpetually.

12. It is a fundamental truth that like Salvation, those who have stepped through "the door" never look back. but are blessed by the ability to have a "direct line" with the Father.

13. You cannot "lose the gift", once given, God does not reclaim it, for the gifts of God are without repentance.

H. Some benefits of speaking/praying in tongues:

1. It becomes your personal means of communicating with God freely.

2. It is a prayer that circumvents our own human reasoning and thinking, because Holy Spirit intercedes on our behalf for us and others. We speak mysteries unto God.

3. It naturally activates and leads unto the other gifts of Holy Spirit. Interpretation, Prophecy, the gift of Tongues and Discerning of spirits, the words of Knowledge and Wisdom.

4. It augments our worship and singing, it focusses us on two levels as we do so – in the spirit and in our understanding.

5. It unites us in corporate worship.

6. It edifies us personally as we exercise the gift.

Father-God, I pray that every person who reads this will be made extremely hungry and thirsty for more of You. Holy Spirit fill the reader with Your Presence, enable them to speak freely to you in their own personal tongue and empower them in Your love to be Your witnesses for Jesus while they are on this earth. In Jesus' name, amen.

Bibliography.

1. MOUNCE, WILLIAM D, *Complete expository Dictionary of Old and New Testament words.* Zondervan, Grand Rapids, Michigan, 2006.
2. VINE, W E. *Vine's complete Expository Dictionary of Old and New testament words.* Thomas Nelson, Nashville, Illinois, 1985.
3. http://www.scripture4all.org/OnlineInterlinear/Greek_Index.htm

35509566R00016

Printed in Poland
by Amazon Fulfillment
Poland Sp. z o.o., Wrocław